WRITING PARAGRAPHS

How to Make Your Writing Great!

WRITING PARAGRAPHS

How to Make Your Writing Great!

Published by
Heron Books, Inc.
20950 SW Rock Creek Road
Sheridan, OR 97378

heronbooks.com

Special thanks to all the teachers and students who
provided feedback instrumental to this edition.

Fifth Edition © 1992, 2021 Heron Books
All Rights Reserved

ISBN: 978-0-89-739150-4

Any unauthorized copying, translation, duplication or distribution, in whole or in part, by any means, including electronic copying, storage or transmission, is a violation of applicable laws.

The Heron Books name and the heron bird symbol are registered trademarks
of Delphi Schools, Inc.

Printed in the USA

10 June 2021

At Heron Books, we think learning should be engaging and fun. It should be hands-on and allow students to move at their own pace.

To facilitate this, we have created a learning guide that will help any student progress through this book, chapter by chapter, with confidence and interest. Also available is *Writing Paragraphs Workbook Activity Answers*.

Get learning guides at
heronbooks.com/learningguides.

For a final exam and *Writing Paragraphs Workbook Activity Answers*, email
teacherresources@heronbooks.com

We would love to hear from you!
Email us at *feedback@heronbooks.com*.

In This Book

ABOUT THIS BOOK 1

1 THE PARTS OF WRITING 3

2 FOUR KINDS OF WORDS
(that you might already know about) 5

    Nouns 5

    Verbs 6

    Adjectives 7

    Adverbs 9

    Making Sentences with
        Nouns, Verbs, Adjectives, Adverbs and Articles 11

3 FOUR MORE KINDS OF WORDS
(that you might *not* already know about) 13

    Pronouns 13

    Conjunctions 16

    Prepositions 17

    Interjections 20

    4 + 4 = 8 22

4 WHAT MAKES A SENTENCE? 23
Subjects and Verbs 24
Moving Subjects 26
Disappearing Subjects 28
Don't Be Fooled 30

5 SENTENCES START AND STOP 35

6 FINALLY, PARAGRAPHS! 39
Why Paragraphs? 39
Messy Paragraphs 40
Getting Organized 41
When to Start a New Paragraph 44

7 SAY WHAT YOU WANT TO SAY 49
Writing Your First Draft 49
Revising 50

8 ONE LAST LOOK 53

9 WRITE, WRITE, WRITE! 55

About this Book

Do you ever write fun and creative stories?

How about essays for school?

Have you ever written a letter, maybe thanking someone for a present or finding out from a student your age what their city is like?

Maybe you've written emails to people you know?

If you've ever been part of a science fair or geography fair, your display probably included a report on what you learned, right?

Have you also done other kinds of writing?

All these kinds of writing give you chances to communicate your ideas. If you can write well, people enjoy reading your stories, essays, letters, emails or reports, and they understand exactly what you wanted to say.

This book was written to help you write well and say exactly what you want to say.

It was written to help you make your writing great!

Are you ready?

The Parts of Writing

To make your writing great, you have to know the different parts of writing and how to put them together.

It's like *building* something or *making* something. You have the different pieces, and you put them together in certain ways.

Have you ever built a model rocket? Have you ever made a fort? Have you ever created a small garden? To make any of these things, you needed the different parts. You needed to know what each one does. And you needed to know how to put them together the right way.

Writing is the same.

The main parts of writing that you need to understand and put together in the right way are:

1. Different kinds of **words**

2. Different kinds of **sentences**

3. Different kinds of **paragraphs**

If you understand these things, you can put them together in the right ways to make great stories, letters, emails, essays and reports!

So, let's start by talking about different kinds of words.

Four Kinds of Words 2
(that you might already know about)

There are different kinds of words. Four of them you might already know about. If any of these are new to you, don't worry. You will be able to practice them as much as you want.

NOUNS

Nouns are words that name a person, place, thing, or idea. Here are some nouns:

book	house	rooster	Mr. Elroy
bike	Alice	alligator	tulip
cat	dinosaur	popsicle	happiness
chair			

Whenever you are talking about people, places, things, or ideas, you are using nouns.

The frogs by the pond were croaking very loudly.

The car ran right into the tree.

That guy lives in my building.

Portland is a small city.

We all use nouns in our writing.

FOUR KINDS OF WORDS

VERBS

Verbs are words that show action (action verbs) or the way something is (being verbs). Here are some action verbs and being verbs:

Action	Action	Action	Being
run	talk	dig	is
jump	sing	pronounce	are
hide	explain	bake	am
			become

Sometimes verbs work together when one verb (called the *helping verb*) helps an action verb. Here are some examples with the helping verb shown in blue:

I can play soccer well.

She is singing.

We will leave tomorrow.

Francesca might talk now.

Sometimes there is more than one helping verb with an action verb.

I will be playing soccer.

He might be leaving soon.

Glory may be talking too much.

Verbs give nouns something to do! Just for fun, try making up some funny sentences using these nouns and verbs in different ways.

nouns	verbs
turtle	talks
arrow	jumps
phone	flies
school	is
happiness	becomes

ADJECTIVES

Adjectives are describing words that tell more about nouns. Here are some examples of adjectives:

silly	clean	flat	huge
purple	careful	circular	clever
beautiful	tall	sad	fun

Adjectives can help make your nouns more interesting. Here are some examples:

crazy helicopter   brilliant sunshine

ridiculous clown   friendly doctor

boring rain   stupid joke

FOUR KINDS OF WORDS

frightened elephant

terrible thunderstorm

Now try mixing up these adjectives and nouns, like *crazy elephant* or *boring joke.* Then try picking your own adjectives to go with each noun.

> ### helpful hint
> When you are writing poetry, try using different nouns and verbs and adjectives together in ways that are unusual.
>
> The handsome mountain shouted, "hello!"
>
> I whispered back, "hello?"
>
> Then the sun screamed at both of us. "Hey, I'm the boss here! Who said you tiny bugs could squeak at each other?"
>
> The mountain and I both ran away like scared chickens.
>
> Using unusual words helps you use your imagination!

Articles

Articles are special adjectives.

There are only three articles:

a   an   the

A and *an* both mean *any one* of the things you are talking about. Usually you use *a*. You only use *an* when the word after it starts with a vowel sound.

a pig	a bush	an egg
a chair	an octopus	an umbrella
a parachute	an iPad	

The means you are talking about a *specific thing or things*. But it doesn't mean *any one*, it means *something specific*.

If you said, "I want *a* book," that means you want *any* book. If you said, "I want *the* book over there with the red and green stripes on the cover," you are saying you want that *specific* book.

Here are more examples of articles:

an apple	the dollar	a photograph
a computer	a dollar	an alligator
the computer	a microscope	the ceiling

ADVERBS

Adverbs are describing words that tell more about verbs, adjectives and other adverbs. They tell *when, where* or *how*. Here are some examples of adverbs:

adverbs describing verbs

run fast	leave soon	jump high
talk slowly	sing loudly	stop here

FOUR KINDS OF WORDS

adverbs describing adjectives

very smart super cool dark red

always careful pretty simple completely flat

adverbs describing other adverbs

very slowly too quickly most especially

awfully loudly more carefully quite happily

helpful hint

When talking, most people say the adverbs *really* and *very* a lot. In your writing, it's better not to use them too much. Sometimes you can just take them out. Sometimes you can find a different word that is just as good, or better!

Not so good: I'm really glad we went to the circus. It was really fun. The clowns were very funny, even though their costumes were really stupid.

Better: I'm so glad we went to the circus. It was super fun. The clowns were especially funny, even though their costumes were stupid.

To make your writing great, don't use *really* and *very* too much.

MAKING SENTENCES WITH NOUNS, VERBS, ADJECTIVES, ADVERBS AND ARTICLES

You can use all these kinds of words to make a sentence. Here are a few examples:

noun   verb   adjective   noun
Frieda loves juicy oranges.

article   noun   adverb   verb   article noun
The teacher quickly taught a lesson.

adjective   noun verb   adverb   adverb
Speedy jets fly really high.

Using these different kinds of words can help you build fun sentences, which is the first step toward the goal of making your writing great!

---

just for fun!

Get another person and read the story below to them by saying a word every place there is a blank. Then have them try it with you!

Whenever _____ wants to _____ with excitement, he/she takes a
              noun (person)   verb

_____ and _____ it all over. Then he/she swings a _____
 noun   verb   noun

and tosses it over _____ river. You _____ wonder why _____
                     article   helping verb   noun (person)

does this. I don't _____ ! _____ is probably just _____ .
                  verb   noun (person)   adjective

If it were me, I would _____ more _____ !
                        verb   adverb

You can then try making up your own fill-in-the-blanks stories. They can be a lot of fun and help you get good at thinking of different nouns, verbs, adjectives, adverbs and articles.

Four More Kinds of Words 3
(that you might *not* already know about)

PRONOUNS

A pronoun is a word that you use in place of a noun.

Here are some examples of pronouns:

he	me	they	her
she	you	it	us
I	we	him	them

Sometimes it sounds funny to keep saying the name of a person, place or thing over and over. That's when you need a pronoun.

Example without pronouns:

> Josef wanted to buy an apple, but only if the apple was green. Josef went to the store and saw lots of apples, but all the apples were red. Josef looked carefully at all the apples. "Yes," Josef said to himself, "there are no green apples here." Josef wasn't very happy. Then suddenly Josef saw the green apple. The apple was the one green apple left. Josef quickly grabbed the apple and went to the cashier to pay for the apple.

FOUR MORE KINDS OF WORDS

Example using pronouns:

> Josef wanted to buy an apple, but only if it was green. He went to the store and saw lots of apples, but they were all red. He looked carefully at them all. "Yes," Josef said to himself, "there are no green apples here." He wasn't very happy. Then suddenly he saw a flash of green! It was the one green apple left! He quickly grabbed it and went to the cashier to pay for it.

The first example sounds a little bit silly because it keeps saying *Josef, Josef, Josef* and *apple, apple, apple*. That's not the way people talk or write.

It's not how you talk, is it?

No, you use pronouns like *he, it, they* and *them* all the time, even if you never noticed before!

The second example sounds much better. Why? Because of pronouns!

When you don't want to keep saying the name of something over and over, pronouns help make it sound right!

Here is another example.

Without pronouns:

> Winnie picked up the stick. Winnie threw the stick over the fence. Then Winnie realized Winnie wanted the stick back. Winnie climbed over the fence to get the stick.

With pronouns:

> Winnie picked up the stick. She threw it over the fence. Then she realized she wanted it back. She climbed over the fence to get it.

FOUR MORE KINDS OF WORDS

For some pronouns, like *you*, *I* and *me*, you just use the pronoun instead of the name.

I hope *you* will give *me* a ticket so *I* can go with *you*.

Imagine that your name is Austin and you are talking to your friend whose name is Lee. Here's how that sentence would sound without pronouns:

Austin hopes Lee will give Austin a ticket so Austin can go with Lee.

It sounds like you're talking about other people, not you and your friend!

Let's write that sentence correctly again:

I hope *you* will give *me* a ticket so *I* can go with *you*.

That sentence really shows how we use pronouns all the time! It has five pronouns and only one noun! (Can you spot the noun in that sentence?)

just for fun!

Try telling someone about what you did yesterday without using any pronouns.

The other person can look at the list of pronouns and give you a loud "beep!" every time you say one of them.

Don't forget that *I* and *me* are pronouns. Trying to say what you did yesterday without saying *I* or *me* is very hard!

If you do it right, it will sound really silly.

Good luck!

FOUR MORE KINDS OF WORDS

CONJUNCTIONS

Conjunctions are words used to connect words or groups of words.

There are lots of conjunctions but just four you probably use the most!

    and   but   or   because

Here are some examples showing how conjunctions connect words and groups of words together.

I love drawing. I love painting.

I love drawing and painting.

Do you like bananas? Do you like strawberries?

Do you like bananas or strawberries?

She wanted to go to town. You left too early.

She wanted to go to town, but you left too early.

We are eating right now. We are starving!

We are eating right now because we are starving!

FOUR MORE KINDS OF WORDS

> ## *helpful hint*
>
> You usually don't want to use more than one or two conjunctions in a sentence.
>
> If you use too many conjunctions, you can end up with something like this:
>
> The woman walked across the street *and* into the store *and* started looking for the red leather purse she'd seen the other day *but* when she found it *and* looked at it closely, she decided she didn't like it *because* it was too small *and* she left.
>
> That sentence is too long!

PREPOSITIONS

Prepositions are words we use to show the relationship between things, like *over*, *under*, *through* and *in*.

Here are a few examples of prepositions that show different relationships between a dog and a table:

The dog jumped *over* the table.

The dog sat *on* the table.

The dog slept *under* the table.

The dog walked *around* the table.

The dog bumped *into* the table.

The dog hid *beneath* the table.

FOUR MORE KINDS OF WORDS

Here are a few examples showing the relationship between a girl and some roses:

The girl looked at the roses.

The girl sat in the roses.

The girl sang to the roses.

The girl walked through the roses.

The girl moved between the roses.

The girl played with the roses.

You use prepositions all the time in your writing. They show where things are in relationship to other things or how things are related or connected.

I learned about cats.

He stood by the door.

The bear is inside the cave.

This is a book on manners.

This gift is for you.

We drove across the bridge.

FOUR MORE KINDS OF WORDS

Try different prepositions used above in these sentences:

The girl got _____ the blanket.

We walked _____ the city.

They sang _____ the rain.

The helicopter flew _____ the sky.

The great thing about prepositions is that you have so many choices!

Here is an alphabetical list of prepositions you can use in your writing. And there are even more prepositions than these!

above	between	onto
according to	by	over
across	during	through
after	for	throughout
around	from	to
at	in	until
before	inside	up to
behind	into	with
below	of	within
beneath	on	without

FOUR MORE KINDS OF WORDS

> ### helpful hint
>
> You probably noticed that some of the prepositions are more than one word that work together to make a preposition.
>
> Sometimes words work like that, even nouns and verbs.
>
> For example, police officer, New York and stop sign are nouns made from two words. We know they are nouns because they name a person, place or thing.
>
> > The police officers in New York will give you a ticket if you don't stop your bike at a stop sign.
>
> An example of a two-word verb is turn in. An example of a three-word verb is look up to. Even though they are more than one word, each is an action verb.
>
> > My friends look up to me because I always turn in my assignments on time.

INTERJECTIONS

Interjections are words that show emotions like surprise, joy or anger.

Here are some examples of interjections:

Wow! That was amazing!

Oh! I didn't know that.

We won! Hurray!

Ouch! That hurt.

Yahoo! We made it!

Oops. I didn't mean that.

Some interjections are small groups of words, like these:

Holy cow! What was that?

My, oh my! What a surprise!

Oh well, we tried.

Uh oh! That wasn't right.

Some interjections sound funny. Old-fashioned ones sound funny to young people. Newer ones sound funny to older people.

Older interjections:

Fiddlesticks! The cat ran off again.

Drat! I stubbed my toe.

My grandkids are coming to visit! Hot dog!

Newer interjections:

Awesome! We have a field trip tomorrow!

The game started and we scored a goal. Boom!

Sweet! My mom said I could go!

Interjections can add strong feelings to your writing. They can help make your writing great! Yay!

FOUR MORE KINDS OF WORDS

4 + 4 = 8

Why are we suddenly doing math when this book is about writing? It's because we had a chapter on "Four Kinds of Words" and we're about to finish this chapter on "Four More Kinds of Words."

4 + 4 = 8

Here are all eight of the different kinds of words we've gone over:

nouns	*pronouns*
verbs	*conjunctions*
adjectives including articles	*prepositions*
adverbs	*interjections*

You can write almost anything in the world using these eight different kinds of words. What's next? Sentences!

---

just for fun!

Here's another fill-in-the-blank game, but this time there are also pronouns, conjunctions, prepositions and interjections!

Get another person and read the story, saying words that can fit in the blanks. Then have them do their own version of the story back to you.

I once knew a _____ _____ named _____ .
            adjective   *noun*   *noun*

_____ loved to _____ popcorn _____ my _____ .
pronoun   *verb*   *preposition*   *noun*

One day, _____ crawled _____ a pond _____ across a _____ .
             noun   *preposition*   *conjunction*   *noun*

_____ ! I couldn't believe how a _____ could _____ so _____ .
interjection   *noun*   *verb*   *adverb*

It was _____ _____ thing to _____ ! After that, I never saw
           article *adjective*   *verb*

_____ again. I am _____ _____ about that!
noun   *adverb* *adjective*

What Makes a Sentence? 4

Now that we've talked about different kinds of *words*, it's time to talk about *sentences*.

A **sentence** is a group of words that tells a whole idea and makes sense.

A sentence has three main parts:

1. A noun or pronoun that tells who or what is doing an action or what the sentence is about.

2. A verb that tells what the noun or pronoun is doing or the way it is.

3. Other words that usually tell more about the noun or pronoun and the verb.

WHAT MAKES A SENTENCE?

SUBJECTS AND VERBS

A sentence *always* has a noun (or pronoun) and a verb. It *usually* has other words that tell more about the noun and verb.

As you know, a noun is a word that names a person, place, thing or idea, and a pronoun is a word that replaces a noun. The noun or pronoun that the sentence is about, and any describing words that go with it, are called the **subject** of the sentence.

Here are examples with the subject nouns (or pronouns) in red and the verbs in blue:

The actor practiced his lines.

I saw a giraffe on the street!

She forgot her glasses.

Mr. Fortune thinks like you.

That serious face finally smiled.

Newts can have an orange belly.

Here are more sentences showing the complete subjects in red and the verbs in blue:

The little artist painted carefully.

My sister, Iris, said you went home.

Jesse loves grilled cheese.

Miss Dawn thanked you.

This football is flat.

Newton the newt can move fast.

Here are more examples:

These pigs will eat anything!

Many tall trees swayed loudly.

Fried eggs taste great.

Dr. Jones was very patient.

WHAT MAKES A SENTENCE?

The time is flying by so fast.   Johnny reads.

Toni came over yesterday   Authors write.

You probably noticed that two of the sentences have *only* a subject and a verb. Those are sentences too. They just don't have any other words that tell more about the subject or the verb.

When you write a question, there is usually a helping verb before the subject and the action or being verb after the subject, like this:

Will the actor practice his lines?   Does Mr. Fortune think like you?

Did I see a giraffe on the street?   Did that serious face finally smile?

Is she forgetting her glasses?   Can newts have an orange belly?

helpful hint

Here's a trick you can use if you aren't sure what the whole verb is in a question.

Change the order of the words so it's not a question anymore but an answer to the question using the same words, just in different order.

If we take the questions above and turn them into answers, they look like this:

The actor will practice his lines.   Mr. Fortune does think like you.

I did see a giraffe on the street.   That serious face finally did smile.

She is forgetting her glasses.   Newts can have an orange belly.

Now the whole verb is easy to see because the parts are right next to each other!

MOVING SUBJECTS

Sometimes the subject moves around in the sentence.

Here's a sentence with the subject at the beginning:

> A big black bear charged out of the woods straight at me!

Okay, that's like most of the sentences we've looked at so far. But what about this one?

> Out of the woods, a big black bear charged straight at me!

The subject moved to the middle of the sentence.

But that's not all a subject can do. Sometimes a subject is at the end of the sentence, like this:

> Out of the woods, straight at me, charged a big black bear!

When you write, you don't always have to put your subject at the beginning of the sentence. Sometimes it's interesting to put the subject in a different place. In the last example above, the reader doesn't find out how scary it is until the very end of the sentence!

Here's another example where you might think putting the subject at the end makes the sentence more interesting:

> A huge spaceship suddenly appeared just 50 feet over my head!

> Just 50 feet over my head, a huge spaceship suddenly appeared!

> Suddenly, just 50 feet over my head, appeared a huge spaceship!

It's usually easier to put your subject first, but it's sometimes fun to move your subjects around!

If you aren't sure where the subject is in a sentence, just ask yourself this question: "Who or what is doing the action or is a certain way?"

Here's an example:

After dinner, Malik likes to have dessert.

Is the subject of this sentence *dinner*? Is it *Malik*? Is it *dessert*?

Well, "Who or what is doing the action *likes*?" Oh, that's obvious. It's Malik. Who likes to have dessert? Malik does. Malik is the subject.

Here's another example:

At the dinner table, my mother is very strict about things.

Is the subject of the sentence *table, mother* or *things*? All of those words are nouns, right? But only one of them is the subject. Who or what is doing the action or is a certain way? If you said *my mother*, you are right! *My mother* is the subject of that sentence.

If the subject is hard to spot, you can always use this "who or what?" question to help you find it.

WHAT MAKES A SENTENCE?

> *just for fun!*
>
> Sometimes there are two subjects that use the same verb, like this:
>
> Tkeisha and I love country music.
>
> Sometimes there are two or more verbs for one subject, like this:
>
> My brother hiked and climbed trees all day.
>
> You can play a simple game with a friend called "2 for the price of 1." Here's how it works:
>
> Your friend says a verb, and you make up a sentence that has two subjects that use that one verb. Then your friend says a subject, and you make up a sentence that has two verbs with that one subject.
>
> Try it! It's a great way to practice subjects and verbs!

DISAPPEARING SUBJECTS

Sometimes a subject doesn't just move, it disappears completely!

Even though the following sentences look like they don't have a subject, they do:

Please sit down.   Watch out for that puddle!

Come in!   Call me later.

The subject that has disappeared in these sentences is the word *you*.

(You) please sit down.   (You) watch out for that puddle!

(You) come in.   (You) call me later.

When you are *telling someone to do something*, the subject disappears.

WHAT MAKES A SENTENCE?

If you turn it into a question, the subject reappears!

> Will you please sit down?
>
> Won't you come in?

> Can you watch out for that puddle?
>
> Can you call me later?

But you don't need to worry much about disappearing subjects. The only time they totally disappear is when you are *telling someone to do something*.

helpful hint

If you ever think you're being too bossy, just listen to the things you are saying to other people. If your sentences have disappearing subjects all the time, you're probably being too bossy! (The subject of the following sentences is *you*.)

> Stop bugging me!
>
> Quit doing that.
>
> Go get your books.
>
> Grab my coat for me.

> Get out of here!
>
> Come over here right now.
>
> Pick up your stuff!
>
> Teach yourself!

The helpful hint is this: try questions instead. "Can you please stop bugging me?" The disappearing *you* has reappeared, and it now sounds more polite. ☺

DON'T BE FOOLED

We've learned that subjects can move around:

>Out of the woods, straight at me, charged a big black bear!

We've learned they can even disappear:

>(You) Watch out for that puddle!

We've learned that there can be two subjects with one verb:

>Tkeisha and I love country music.

There can also be two or more verbs with one subject:

>My brother hiked and screamed and yelled at us.

We have seen that there can be lots of other words telling more about the subject or the verb:

>At the dinner table, my mother is very strict about things.

We've also seen sentences that have *only* a subject and a verb.

>Authors write.

What's true about all these different kinds of sentences is they always have a noun (or pronoun) and a verb.

It's a rule about sentences:

>*Sentences always have a noun (or pronoun) and a verb.*

WHAT MAKES A SENTENCE?

But do you remember what a sentence is?

A **sentence** is a group of words that tells a whole idea and makes sense.

Sometimes you can be fooled by a group of words that has a noun and a verb, but *it doesn't tell a whole idea,* or *it doesn't make sense.*

Here are some examples of groups of words that aren't sentences even though each group of words has one or more nouns or pronouns (in red) and one or more verbs (in blue).

If it rains

Because I am happy

When you and Steph walk across the street

Like someone dancing really fast

Talking like every other person here

Jumping and bouncing down the path

There's at least one noun and one verb in all these groups of words. But they aren't sentences. Can you tell why?

It's because these groups of words don't tell a whole idea. If you say them out loud, you can probably tell they don't sound quite right. They need more words to make sense.

Let's add some words to make them into *whole ideas that make sense*:

If it rains, we will go to the park.

I'm smiling because I am happy.

WHAT MAKES A SENTENCE?

When you and Steph walk across the street, you look like brothers.

He shook his arms like someone dancing really fast.

Jeff is talking like every other person here.

The ball went jumping and bouncing down the path.

If you write a group of words that tells a complete idea and sounds right, it's probably a sentence.

But don't be fooled. If it doesn't sound quite right or if it sounds like it needs more words to make sense, it's probably not really a sentence. Usually it's because you accidentally broke a sentence in two, like this:

If it rains. We will go to the park.

I'm smiling. Because I am happy.

When you and Steph walk across the street. You look like brothers.

He shook his arms. Like someone dancing really fast.

When you accidentally break a sentence in two, your writing is not so great. People get confused because what you've written doesn't quite make sense.

To make your writing great, make sure your sentences have a subject and a verb, and make sure they sound right and make sense!

WHAT MAKES A SENTENCE?

> ### helpful hint
>
> There is actually one special kind of sentence that doesn't have a subject *or* a verb. Can you think of what kind of sentence that is?
>
> It's when you use an interjection.
>
> > Whoa! Francisco jumped!
>
> The first sentence just has an interjection. The second sentence is more the regular kind of sentence. It has a subject (Francisco) and a verb (jumped).
>
> So, if someone (like this book) tells you that every sentence has to have a subject and a verb, you can say, "Excuse me, but that's not exactly true! Have you ever heard of an interjection?"

Sentences Start and Stop 5

A sentence starts, tells a whole idea, and then stops. That seems easy enough but sometimes it can be tricky.

Have you ever seen (or written) a sentence like this?

> I went to the store to buy a new skateboard while I was there, I met my friend Kamal, who is the funniest person I know, he was hungry so we decided to get something to eat, we went to our favorite pizza place and got lunch.

That's tough to read! Why? It has a lot of complete ideas all jammed together into one sentence.

There's a name for this kind of sentence that just goes on and on and on. It's called a **run-on sentence**. It is two or more complete sentences stuck together with commas instead of conjunctions or with no punctuation at all. Run-on sentences need to be broken up into smaller parts that make sense, and each part needs to stop.

How do you stop a sentence? With three different **punctuation marks**, of course. You use a *period* (.) for a regular sentence. You use a *question mark* (?) when it's asking a question. And when you want to show strong feeling, you use an *exclamation point* (!), which is sometimes called an *exclamation mark*.

SENTENCES START AND STOP

So, let's try one more time to write about the new skateboard, Kamal and eating pizza, but using punctuation marks to stop each sentence.

> *I went to the store to buy a new skateboard. While I was there, I met Kamal, who is the funniest person I know! He was hungry so we decided to get something to eat. We went to our favorite pizza place and got lunch.*

That's a lot easier to read! It doesn't have any run-on sentences in it.

This doesn't mean you can't have two ideas in the same sentence. Here are two examples of good sentences that each have two ideas in them:

> *I usually get hungry about 11 AM, so I go get a piece of fruit.*

> *I was hiking through the woods when I saw a huge elk.*

Those are fine. The ideas go together, and the sentences sound right.

But what about this one?

> *I enjoy going to school each morning we study math first.*

That one doesn't work. It doesn't sound right. It has two separate ideas jammed together with no punctuation. It's a run-on sentence.

Here's one way to fix it:

> *I enjoy going to school each morning. We study math first.*

You could also use a conjunction to connect them, like this:

> *I enjoy going to school each morning because we study math first.*

SENTENCES START AND STOP

You might even be able to think of another way to make it work. You just have to make sure each sentence tells a whole idea, and it sounds right!

> ### helpful hint
>
> There's a simple trick you can use for fixing super long run-on sentences:
>
> *Underline every main idea.*
>
> Here's an example of a super-long, run-on sentence. We've underlined every main idea in it.
>
> > <u>I like crackers</u>, <u>when I get hungry in the morning I go get some crackers and butter</u> this <u>makes me late for class and the teacher always wants to know where I've been,</u> <u>this usually reminds me how much I like crackers,</u> which <u>is something I discovered at summer camp where everyone learned to make a cracker and butter sandwich,</u> <u>I love them!</u>
>
> That's six different main ideas in one sentence! That's a super-long, run-on sentence, for sure!
>
> Here's what to do next. Make every sentence be only one or two main ideas. It might go like this:
>
> > I like crackers. When I get hungry in the morning, I go get some crackers and butter. Sometimes that makes me late for class and the teacher wants to know where I've been. That just reminds me how much I like my cracker and butter sandwiches that I learned to make at summer camp. My problem is I love them!
>
> There are other ways you could fix that super-long, run-on sentence. The trick is to underline the main ideas, then make each sentence have only one or two main ideas.
>
> If you ever have trouble with super-long, run-on sentences, you'll like this trick.

Finally, Paragraphs!

Now that you know about different kinds of words and how sentences are put together, we can finally talk about paragraphs!

A **paragraph** is a group of sentences about one main idea. A paragraph can be just one or two sentences, or it can be three or more. Long or short, it doesn't matter as long as the sentences are well organized.

WHY PARAGRAPHS?

The main reason for paragraphs is to organize your ideas and make it easier for your reader to follow what you're saying.

You might write about a family vacation like this:

> *My family and I took a trip to New York last fall. There were a lot of awesome things about our trip, but the best was getting to see the Statue of Liberty. I've read about it but never knew you could climb the stairs all the way up to the top. The whole experience was amazing. One part of the trip I didn't like was waiting in line for the boat that took us out to the statue. The day was hot, there were crowds of people, and I was hungry! We had to wait for almost an hour. That part wasn't fun. I have to say though, even with the crowds and the wait, the trip was awesome!*

FINALLY, PARAGRAPHS!

It sounds like you had a great time but it's hard to read all the way through. Let's try some paragraphs.

My family and I took a trip to New York last fall.

There were a lot of awesome things about our trip, but the best was getting to see the Statue of Liberty. I've read about it but never knew you could climb the stairs all the way up to the top. The whole experience was amazing.

One part of the trip I didn't like was waiting in line for the boat that took us out to the statue. The day was hot, there were crowds of people, and I was hungry! We had to wait for almost an hour. That part wasn't fun.

I have to say though, even with the crowds and the wait, the trip was awesome!

That's easier to read. Each paragraph talks about a different main idea. The spaces between the paragraphs make the ideas easier to follow, one after the other. It's even nicer to look at!

MESSY PARAGRAPHS

How do you collect sentences into groups of main ideas? Obviously, you won't want to make a paragraph with different ideas all mixed up. You'll end up with a messy paragraph.

It's like this: When your room is a mess, *you* might be able to find things. But if you sent someone else into your room to find something, they probably would come back and say, "Your room is a mess. I couldn't possibly find anything in there!"

It's the same with paragraphs. Maybe *you* know where you put all the ideas, but someone trying to read a messy paragraph just gets lost.

Here's an example of two very messy paragraphs:

> *Shortly after he got there, he saw the moon come up over the swamp. By the time the car was fixed, it was time for lunch. Joe's day didn't go very well. He gave up and drove home and went to bed hungry.*
>
> *However, there wasn't enough food, so he decided to go hunting. The car wouldn't start so he couldn't go to work. He saw lots of animals but wasn't sure whether they would be good to eat. He got in the car, which was running fine now, and drove out. He decided to hunt in the swamp, but it didn't work out very well.*

The sentences are all mixed up. The paragraphs don't make any sense. They need to get organized into main ideas.

GETTING ORGANIZED

There are lots of ways to group your ideas into paragraphs.

For example, if you're writing an essay on what your friends like most about camping trips, you might start out with a short paragraph that tells what you are going to talk about. You then make each paragraph about the main ideas your different friends talked about.

FINALLY, PARAGRAPHS!

I asked my friends to tell me what they like best about summer camping trips. Here's what they had to say.

Sally and Kenji are all about the food. They like the hot dogs, hamburgers and desserts, especially the s'mores. Sally says she really doesn't care where we camp as long as there are plenty of hot dogs and marshmallows!

Jake, Samir and Ellie look for a place with lots of water. They like swimming, wading and splash fights. Ellie also likes playing soccer on the beach by the ocean.

Campfires every night are what make camping fun for Alia and Jackie. They love toasting marshmallows and telling scary stories around the fire.

Funny thing though, all my friends hate one thing about camping. Rain! If it rains, they would all rather be anywhere than in a tent!

Let's try a different example. In this one, you are writing about different kinds of snack foods and how popular they are. You decide to organize your paragraphs so that each one talks about a different kind of snack food. After a paragraph that starts things off, each kind of snack food will be a main idea and will get its own paragraph.

I asked the people in my class to tell me what they think about snack food. They sure had a lot of opinions!

Pizza was a popular choice for snacks. From small cheese pizzas to giant, five-topping pizzas, there wasn't much they didn't like. Most of the class thought plain cheese pizza would be the best choice for a class treat. Almost everyone likes it and you don't have to argue over toppings.

Another snack everyone liked is popcorn. It's crunchy, salty, buttery, and so good. Almost everyone agreed that the very best popcorn is the kind you get at the movies, except Sammy. She likes her grandmother's popcorn much more than any other kind.

My own favorite snack is raisins covered with yogurt. It's been my favorite snack since I was little. Nobody else I talked to likes my favorite snack, but that didn't change my mind.

Another easy way to organize paragraphs, especially when you are writing a story, is to put them in order of what happened. Each paragraph tells a very small part of the story. Here's an example.

When Phillip was very young, he dreamed of being an astronaut. He wanted to fly in a spaceship to outer space and discover new planets. All he ever talked about was spaceships, planets, moons and stars.

After starting school, he got interested in sports. He played kickball first. Then he started playing soccer, which he loved even more. By the time he was ten, he was convinced he wanted to be a professional soccer player.

Then one day, in junior high, he discovered taekwondo from a friend. Taekwondo is a martial art, like karate and judo. The thing that is different about taekwondo is that you use a lot of different kicks. Isn't it interesting that he always liked to kick things? First it was kickballs, then it was soccer balls, then it was people!

Now that he is grown, he still plays soccer and practices taekwondo, but now he works as a violin teacher. He is my violin teacher! Sometimes when I go to lessons, we talk about other things. That's how I learned all about his life.

FINALLY, PARAGRAPHS!

The first paragraph talks about when Phillip was very young. The next one talks about when he was a bit older. The next one talks about when he was a teenager. The last one talks about when he was an adult.

There are many ways you can organize paragraphs, just like there are many ways to organize your room. The important thing is to clean up any messy paragraphs and try to make each paragraph about one main idea.

WHEN TO START A NEW PARAGRAPH

You can usually tell when it's time to start a new paragraph. It's when you are ready to write about a different main idea.

Take a look at this short report about cats:

Cats are furry, four-legged mammals. They have long whiskers and sharp teeth. Most cats weigh between 10 and 15 pounds, but some are larger. Cats that go outdoors like to hunt small animals like mice and birds. Indoor cats like to play with balls, string and small stuffed toys. No matter whether they live outdoors or indoors, cats spend a lot of their time sleeping.

Can you tell where the first main idea stops and a new one begins? It's where the writer stops talking about what cats look like and begins talking about what they do. Let's take a look at the same report separated into paragraphs.

Cats are furry, four-legged mammals. They have long whiskers and sharp teeth. Most cats weigh between 10 and 15 pounds, but some are larger.

FINALLY, PARAGRAPHS!

> *Cats that go outdoors like to hunt small animals like mice and birds. Indoor cats like to play with balls, string and small stuffed toys. No matter whether they live outdoors or indoors, cats like to spend a lot of their time sleeping.*

Breaking it up this way makes each idea easier to understand.

Here's another example:

> *My favorite thing to do on a summer day is read. I like nothing better than hanging out under a tree with a cold lemonade and a great book. Reading takes me to places I have never been. It sends me on wild adventures and into scary mysteries. I've gone to Mars, found hidden treasure, dived to the bottom of the ocean and learned more about what's in my own backyard. Reading a good book while listening to the birds and enjoying the shade is my idea of a good time in the summer!*

There are three main ideas all squished together. Can you say what they are?

Let's write this again, but this time we'll start a new paragraph when we switch to a new main idea.

> *My favorite thing to do on a summer day is read. I like nothing better than hanging out under a tree with a cold lemonade and a great book.*
>
> *Reading takes me to places I have never been. It sends me on wild adventures and into scary mysteries. I've gone to Mars, found hidden treasure, dived to the bottom of the ocean and learned more about what's in my own backyard.*
>
> *Reading a good book while listening to the birds and enjoying the shade is my idea of a good time in the summer!*

FINALLY, PARAGRAPHS!

Sometimes you can start a new paragraph when you switch from talking about good things to talking about some bad things. Let's use the example about the trip to the Statue of Liberty from the very beginning of the chapter.

My family and I took a trip to New York last fall.

There were a lot of awesome things about our trip but the best was getting to see the Statue of Liberty. I've read about it but never knew you could climb the stairs all the way up to the top. The whole experience was amazing.

One part of the trip I didn't like was waiting in line for the boat that took us out to the statue. The day was hot, there were crowds of people, and I was hungry! We had to wait for almost an hour. That part wasn't fun.

I have to say though, even with the crowds and the wait, the trip was awesome!

The first paragraph just gets the reader started. The second is about the best part of the trip. The third paragraph is about the not-so-good part of the trip. And the last paragraph wraps it all up. The reader can easily move along through the different ideas to the end.

You can see that there are lots of different ways you can organize your paragraphs. And you can usually tell when it's time to start a new one because you are starting to talk about a new main idea.

There isn't any *perfect* way to organize your writing into paragraphs. The important thing is that your paragraphs help your reader follow your ideas and enjoy your writing!

helpful hint

There are actually three different ways you can show the beginning of a new paragraph!

1. Leave a blank line between one paragraph and the next:

    Cats are furry, four-legged mammals. They have long whiskers and sharp teeth. Most cats weigh between 10 and 15 pounds, but some are larger.

    Many people like to keep cats for pets instead of dogs. Cats don't require as much attention as dogs and they clean up after themselves, which is nice.

2. **Indent** the new paragraph by beginning the first line about a quarter inch further in than the rest of the lines:

    Cats are furry, four-legged mammals. They have long whiskers and sharp teeth. Most cats weigh between 10 and 15 pounds, but some are larger.
    Many people like to keep cats for pets instead of dogs. Cats don't require as much attention as dogs and they clean up after themselves, which is nice.

3. Indent and leave a space:

    Cats are furry, four-legged mammals. They have long whiskers and sharp teeth. Most cats weigh between 10 and 15 pounds, but some are larger.

    Many people like to keep cats for pets instead of dogs. Cats don't require as much attention as dogs and they clean up after themselves, which is nice.

This book uses the first way. Which way you do it is up to you!

Say What You Want to Say

When you write, you want your communication to be clear and easy for your reader to understand. You want clear sentences and well-organized paragraphs.

This doesn't always happen on your first or second try. Sometimes, it takes more work.

When you write an essay, a report or even a story, you may make several versions before you finally have a really clear communication you are happy with.

The versions you make while writing are called **drafts**.

WRITING YOUR FIRST DRAFT

To get started, you write a **first draft**.

In your first draft, you simply try to get your thoughts down in writing without trying to make it perfect. There might be some mistakes in your words or sentences. There might be problems with your paragraphs. It might not communicate everything you want to say.

That's ok. It isn't finished yet.

SAY WHAT YOU WANT TO SAY

REVISING

Now it's time for revising. When you **revise** writing, you make changes to improve it.

The first step is to simply read over what you wrote. While you read, try to look at the writing as if you had never seen it before.

Does it say what you want it to say? Is it easy to understand?

How about the sentences? Are there incomplete sentences or run-on sentences?

Do the paragraphs make sense? Is there anything missing? Do they seem to be in the best order?

After you read over your writing, it's time to revise anything that wasn't quite right.

You might decide to change a few sentences to make them communicate better or even re-organize a whole paragraph. You might add more information. You do whatever is needed to make it an even clearer communication.

Next, you write a new draft with all your revisions. This is your **second draft**.

Are you done now?

Maybe, maybe not. Read it over again and see what you think. Could you make it better? If so, do it! Keep revising and re-writing until you have a paragraph or story that you are happy to give to your reader.

Here's a short list of things you can check when it's time to revise your writing:

- Are there incomplete sentences or run-on sentences?
- Does each sentence communicate clearly?
- Do the paragraphs make sense?
- Have I left anything out?

The goal is to end up with great writing that <u>says what you want it to say</u>!

helpful hint

It can be hard to get a fresh look at your writing if you have already read it over many times. Here are some things that can help.

1. Put your writing away for a bit. When you read it later, you will see it with a "fresh eye."

2. Read your writing aloud, slowly, listening to how it sounds. Many writers find this helps them spot things that need to be improved.

3. Give your writing to someone else and ask them to tell you what they think. Does it make sense? Does anything need to be clearer? Is there anything confusing?

(If you are writing for school, ask your teacher first if it's ok to have someone else read it before turning it in. Even if they say "yes," it's important that all the writing is *yours* and that nobody else is writing some part of your assignment. You just want them to answer questions like the ones under #3.)

One Last Look

So, you're all done with your writing. The sentences are great! The paragraphs are organized! It says what you want it to say! You're all done, right?

Well, maybe. But there's one last thing to do.

The last step in creating a great paragraph or story is to look it over carefully to make sure there are no mistakes. This is called *proofreading*. And it's different from revising.

When you **proofread**, you are looking over what you've written to make sure there are no little mistakes. You're doing a final, careful check to make sure you didn't miss anything.

To proofread something, you read it over fully, just as though you had never seen it before.

- Look for spelling errors and fix them.

- Look for punctuation and capitalization errors and fix them.

- Look for handwriting or typing errors and fix them.

If there are certain mistakes you make a lot (like mixing up *their* and *they're* or misspelling *receive*), you can add a step to look for and fix those.

The idea is to end up with writing that is easy to read and your reader will enjoy.

ONE LAST LOOK

> *helpful hint*
>
> When you proofread, you can check for different things all at the same time, but some people do best by checking one thing at a time.
>
> For example,
>
> 1. Go through your writing looking for spelling errors and fix what you find.
>
> 2. Go through it again looking for punctuation mistakes.
>
> 3. Then go through it looking for handwriting or typing mistakes, and how it looks overall.
>
> Some writers even read each sentence one at a time but starting from the end of the sentence and reading each word back to the beginning of the sentence! It may sound like a crazy idea, but it can be a great way to find mistakes.
>
> Find what works best for you!

Write, Write, Write!

Wow! You've learned a lot in this book!

You learned about different kinds of words and how to use them to say exactly what you want to say.

You learned about sentences and how to write a great one. You even learned about some odd kinds of sentences!

You learned about paragraphs and how to use them to organize your writing.

Finally, you learned how to make sure your writing says all that you want it to say and looks great!

You're all set to write great essays, letters and stories.

Here's one final piece of advice:

Keep writing! Write short paragraphs and long ones. Write about what you see and what you imagine. Write for others to read, or just for yourself.

But whatever you write about, keep writing!

With practice, you will get better and better at making your writing great!

www.ingramcontent.com/pod-product-compliance
Lightning Source LLC
Chambersburg PA
CBHW050504110426
42742CB00018B/3370